MW00954795

SMOKEJUMPERS ONE to TEN

CHRIS L. DEMAREST

Margaret K. McElderry Books

NEW YORK · LONDON · TORONTO · SYDNEY · SINGAPORE

For Chuck Sheley,
whose tireless and enthusiastic support made this book happen

Acknowledgments

I would like to thank all the personnel at the Redding, California, Jump Base and Arlen Cravins, Base Manager, for giving me free reign to explore and hang out with them. Short of being on the front line, I was given the opportunity to experience their dedication to jumping fire, and I appreciate all the hard work they put into it. May every season be a safe one. And thanks to my editor, Emma Dryden, who caught the smokejumping fever and made this book a far better one than I would have made on my own.

Margaret K. McElderry Books
An imprint of Simon & Schuster Children's Publishing Division
1230 Avenue of the Americas, New York, NY 10020

The text of this book is set in HTF Champion.
The illustrations are rendered in pastels.

Printed in Hong Kong
2 4 6 8 10 9 7 5 3 1
Library of Congress Cataloging-in-Publication Data

Demarest, Chris L.
Smokejumpers One to Ten / Chris L. Demarest.—1st ed.
p. cm.
Includes bibliographical references.
ISBN 0-689-84120-5
1. Smokejumpers—Juvenile literature. 2. Wildfire fighters—Juvenile literature. [1. Smokejumpers.
2. Wildfire fighters. 3. Fire fighters. 4. Occupations. 5. Counting.] I. Title.

SD421.23 .D46 2002
634.9'618—dc21

2001030853

FIRST
EDITION

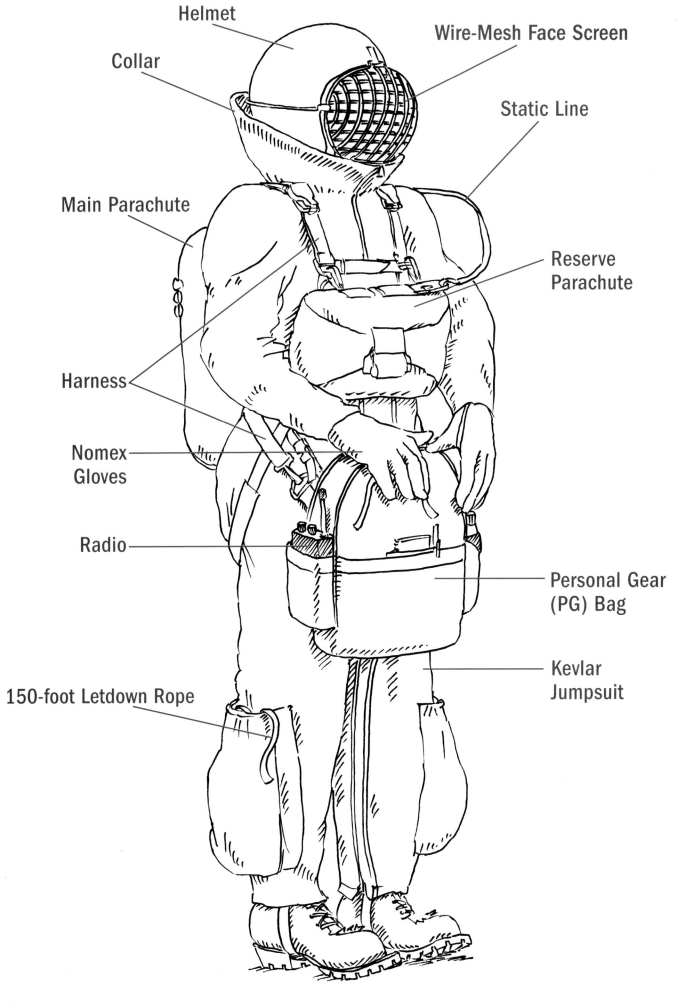

Helmet

Collar

Wire-Mesh Face Screen

Static Line

Main Parachute

Reserve Parachute

Harness

Nomex Gloves

Radio

Personal Gear (PG) Bag

150-foot Letdown Rope

Kevlar Jumpsuit

Smokejumper Outfit

1 ONE lightning bolt, in a flash, strikes a tree.

2 **TWO** pilots radio in what they see.

3 THREE rings, the dispatcher answers the call.

4 FOUR eager smokejumpers race down the hall.

5 FIVE prop blades spin when the pilot calls, "Clear!"

6 SIX crew members take off. Up go the gear.

7 "SEVEN minutes till drop," the pilot calls out.

8 EIGHT restless boots then start moving about.

9 NINE-inch-wide streamers check wind drift below.

10 **TEN** seconds later . . . the *slap*, which means "GO!"

9 NINE acres of towering conifers burn.

8 **EIGHT** rugged hands make the parachutes turn.

7 SEVEN loads of cargo are dropped onto the scene.

6 SIX steps apart, ’jumpers scrape the ground clean.

5 FIVE tugs, the "misery whip" goes to work.

4 FOUR hard hats watch the tree snap with a jerk.

3 THREE drops of slurry help slow the fire's spread.

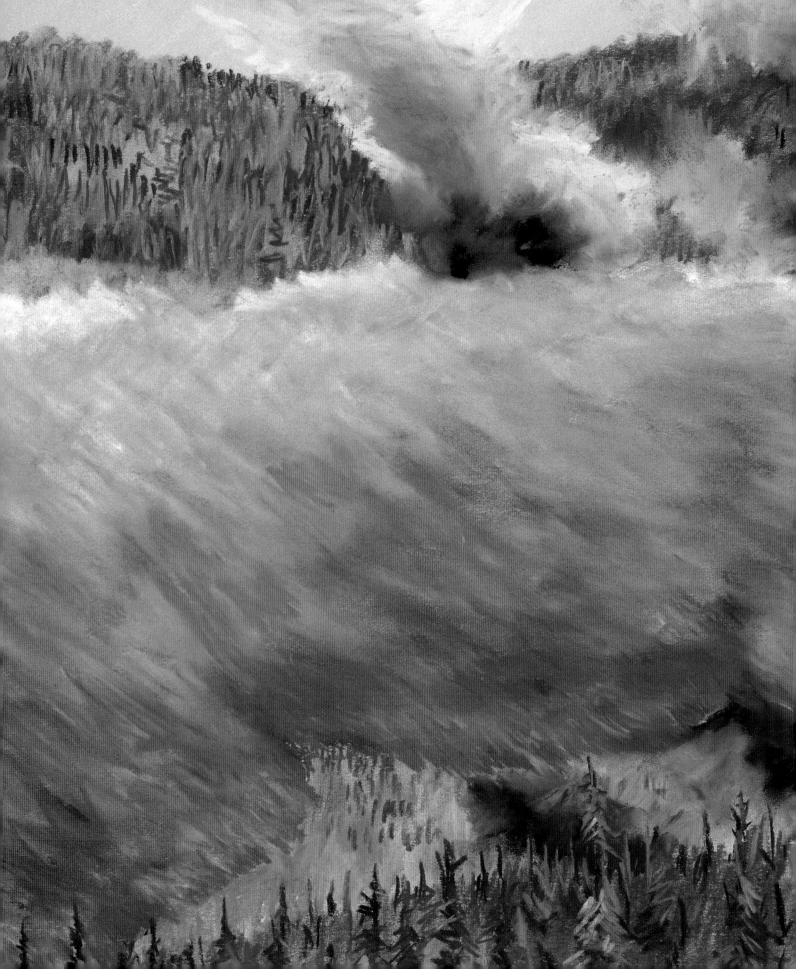

2 TWO days of tough work. The fire is dead.

1 ONE long packout to a rendezvous place.

0

ZERO fires spotted as they fly back to base.

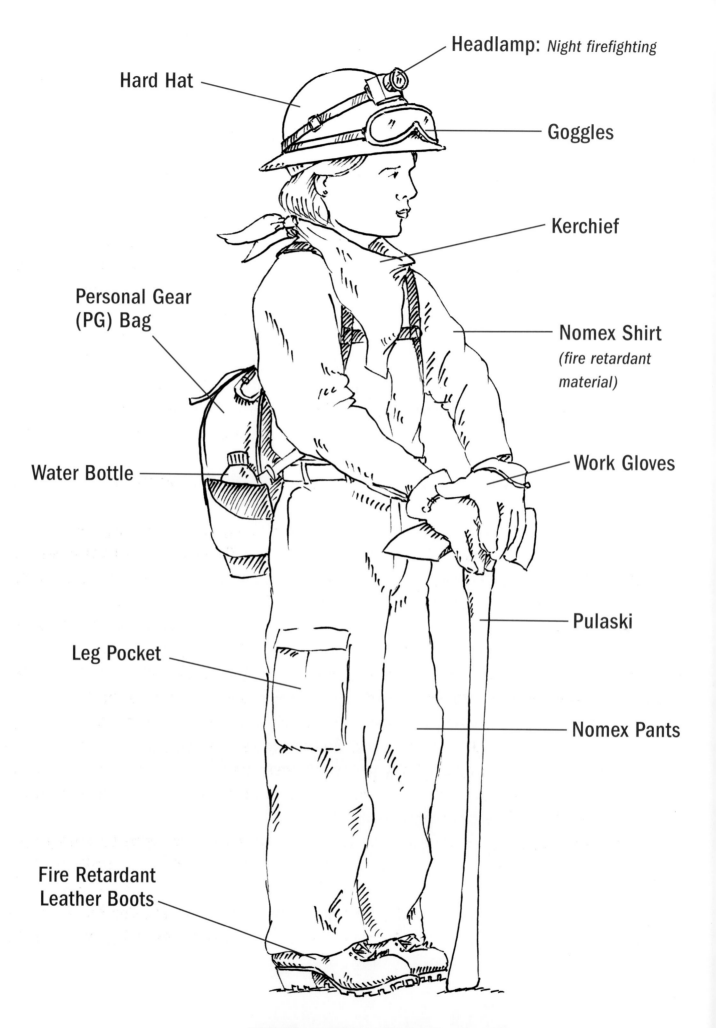

Headlamp: *Night firefighting*

Hard Hat

Goggles

Kerchief

Personal Gear (PG) Bag

Nomex Shirt
(fire retardant material)

Water Bottle

Work Gloves

Pulaski

Leg Pocket

Nomex Pants

Fire Retardant Leather Boots

Wildland Firefighter Outfit

AUTHOR'S NOTE

If left alone, forest fires and wildland fires would burn thirty million acres of land in the United States each year. Smokejumpers are an elite group of wildland firefighters whose task is to parachute into remote areas and contain a fire before it gets out of control.

A little over sixty years have passed since the first smokejumpers dropped from a plane onto a fire scene. Until then, forest firefighters, known as smokechasers, sometimes had to hike several days to reach remote fires. In 1940, after a year of experimenting, the forest service successfully dropped two smokejumpers onto a fire. With smokejumping still in its infancy and with World War II breaking out in 1939, concern grew over the continued protection of the national forests. Since most smokejumpers had joined the armed forces, only a thin smokejumping crew was available. The ranks were filled by conscientious objectors (people who refused to fight in any war) and, later in the war, by an all-Black parachute infantry, which was known as the 555s or the Triple Nickels. This airborne battalion fought thirty-six fires and made over 1,200 jumps and, together with the conscientious objectors, kept the smokejumper program alive during the 1940s. Today, there are about four hundred active smokejumpers. Many compete for open spots, but to first qualify as a smokejumper, a person must have a minimum of two years of wildland fire-fighting experience.

Most fires in vast forested landscapes are started by lightning. When a lightning bolt strikes a tree, it does so with such force that a tree can literally explode. The temperature inside a tree can reach as high as 50,000 degrees Fahrenheit so that the sap instantly boils. Fire can actually smolder for days inside a tree or its root system before it erupts into flame.

When a fire is reported, a plane filled with smokejumpers and a pilot, copilot, and spotter takes off. Once the fire has been located, the spotter finds the safest jump spot for the jumpers and their supplies and drops colored streamers to determine the wind's direction. This will let the spotter know how the smokejumpers' parachutes will drift as they descend to the jump spot.

It's impossible for all the smokejumpers to exit the plane at once and hit their target, so they jump in groups of two, referred to as "sticks." A plane makes several passes over the jump site until all the smokejumpers are out. When all jumpers are on the ground, the plane drops down to treetop level and the spotter shoves out boxes of supplies attached to parachutes. Supplies include everything from food to tools.

There have been only a few parachute accidents in the history of smokejumping, but every jumper carries a reserve chute clipped to the front of their harness as a backup in the rare event that the main chute malfunctions. Most injuries, if any, occur during some phase of the smokejumpers' landing.

Smokejumpers wear heavily padded suits made of a bulletproof material called Kevlar and helmets with wire-mesh face screens to protect them from branches and rocks during their landings.

Each smokejumper carries in one of their leg pockets a 150-foot "letdown rope," which is their means of lowering themselves to the ground if their parachute becomes entangled in a tree. Once they've landed, smokejumpers shed their jumpsuits and helmets to work in the fire-retardant shirts and pants they are wearing underneath. From "Personal Gear," or PG, bags clipped below the reserve chute, they take their work gloves and hard hats. The PG bags then double as backpacks to hold water, food, extra clothing, and two-way radios for communication.

Because smokejumpers carry only enough water for drinking, they have to be clever in how they fight a fire. The classic tool of their trade is a cross between an ax and a hoe, known as a Pulaski, named for its inventor Edward Pulaski, who was a Forest Service ranger in the early 1900s. The hoe end of the tool is used to scrape the ground clean of "duff," a small kindling type of ground cover. By clearing away this material, a "fire break" is created. Several feet wide and running the perimeter of the fire, this break robs the fire of necessary fuel, thereby helping to stop the fire's progress. Some jumpers also use a chain saw or a crosscut saw, which is also known as a "misery whip." The tools that are dropped into the fire scene must be carried out on the backs of the smokejumpers, so many jumpers prefer to use the "misery whip" because it weighs so much less than a chain saw and the fuel needed to run it.

Every firefighter carries with them a fire shelter, or what's commonly referred to as a "Shake 'n Bake." This thin, reflective, aluminum-coated tent is designed to be pulled over the firefighter if he or she is caught in a fast-approaching fire. It can protect a person from being burned in temperatures up to 1,000 degrees Fahrenheit for up to two minutes. Unfortunately, it is no guarantee of survival, and it is used only as a last resort. Most smokejumpers prefer to use their training and knowledge of fire science to avoid having to deploy the shelters.

Today smokejumpers are aided in their battle against wildfires by a liquid, fire-retardant chemical commonly referred to as "slurry." Dropped ahead of the blaze from airplanes, the red-dyed slurry coats the vegetation, thus slowing a fire's progress. Its red color makes it easier for the pilots to keep track of where they've made their drops. Slurry is sometimes dropped from helicopters, but most firefighting helicopters are equipped with a "drop bucket," a large container that hangs below the belly of the craft. It is filled with water that can be dumped directly on a fire.

When a fire is finally out, the "packout" begins. Smokejumpers carry out every piece of equipment, food, clothing, jump gear, and garbage from the area in which they've been working. During a packout, which can take several miles, it is common for each smokejumper to carry close to his or her own weight on their back.

Smokejumping and fighting fires are seasonal occupations. With cooler fall temperatures, the chance of lightning strikes dwindles to almost nothing. With no fires to fight, there is no need for smokejumpers to stay on at a jump base. However, with more undeveloped land with few or no access roads being set aside for conservation reasons, the potential for bigger, longer-lasting fires grows. And with that the need for more smokejumpers and ground crew also grows. Recently, more smokejumpers have been hired as full-time employees. Because of their tree-climbing ability, they sometimes take on more scientific projects in the off-season. This can range from gathering pinecones for study to building roosts for larger birds to, most recently, helping in the fight against the Asian Longhorned Beetle in the urban parks of New York and Chicago.

Every jump base is equipped with several sewing machines, and almost every smokejumper knows how to use one. Except for the parachutes and the fire-retardant shirt and pants which are issued to them, the smokejumpers make their own jumpsuits and PG bags, and repair any damaged parachutes. Before parachutes are repacked, a careful inspection is made. After the repacking, the "rigger" signs off by documenting who packed the chute and the day it was put back into service.

Safety is paramount. Because of their small numbers, smokejumpers become part of what they call their "brotherhood." Today this includes women, too. They work together, look out for each other, and take care of their "bros" as they fight wildland fires to protect people, animals, and the environment.

My interest in smokejumping goes back to my childhood when I was enthralled by the TV show *Ripcord* and fascinated as I watched in person an international parachuting competition. Years later Norman MacLean's book, *Young Men and Fire,* about the Mann Gulch fire of 1949, brought back my interest in smokejumpers.

Smokejumpers One to Ten is a tribute to the men and women who jump fires, as well as to the pilots and all the ground personnel who work fighting fires. And to the families who have lost loved ones in the line of duty, may this be a tribute to their memory.

—C. L. D.

References

Cohen, Stan. *A Pictorial History of Smokejumping*. Missoula, Montana: Pictorial Histories Publishing Company, 1983.

"Firestorm: The Smokejumpers' Story." The Discovery Channel. Bethesda, Maryland, 1999. [video]

"Smokejumpers: Firefighters from the Sky." National Smokejumper Association (NSA). Missoula, Montana, 2000. [video]

Thoele, Michael. *Fire Line: The Summer Battles of the West*. Golden, Colorado: Fulcrum Publishing, 1995.

Suggested Reading

Maclean, John N. *Fire on the Mountain: The True Story of the South Canyon Fire*. New York: William Morrow and Company, 1999.

MacLean, Norman. *Young Men and Fire: A True Story of the Mann Gulch Fire*. Chicago, Illinois: University of Chicago Press, 1992.

Taylor, Murry A. *Jumping Fire: A Smokejumper's Memoir of Fighting Wildfire in the West*. New York: Harcourt, 1999.

Smokejumper magazine (Quarterly). National Smokejumper Association (NSA). Missoula, Montana.

Suggested Web Site

Visit the National Smokejumper Association (NSA) Web site at www.smokejumpers.com.